## HEALTHY AND HAPPY

# Safe and Healthy

Robyn Hardyman

**PowerKiDS** press.

New York

Published in 2012 by The Rosen Publishing Group Inc.
29 East 21st Street, New York, NY 10010

First Edition

Produced for Wayland by Calcium
Design: Paul Myerscough and Geoff Ward
Editor: Sarah Eason
Editor for Wayland: Joyce Bentley
Illustrations: Geoff Ward
Picture Research: Maria Joannou
Consultant: Sue Beck, MSc, BSc

Library of Congress Cataloging-in-Publication Data

Hardyman, Robyn.
Safe and healthy / By Robyn Hardyman. — 1st. ed.
      pages cm. — (Healthy and Happy)
Includes index.
ISBN 978-1-4488-5278-9 (library binding)
1.  Children's accidents—Prevention—Juvenile literature. 2.  Health behavior in
children—Juvenile literature.  I. Title.
HV675.5.H36 2012
613.6—dc22
                                    2010046298

Photographs: Dreamstime: Joseph Helfenberger 6; Istockphoto: Debi Bishop 12, Dejan
Ristovski 21; Shutterstock: Apollofoto 25, Stacy Barnett 2, 11, Galina Barskaya 10,
Andrey Bayda 9, Ronald Caswell 17, Leonid and Anna Dedukh 22, Sandra G. 18, Ilya D.
Gridnev 15, Jack Hollingsworth 26, K Photography 20, Jouke van Keulen 13, Liga
Lauzuma 23, Monkey Business Images 24, Vanessa Nel 16, Thomas M. Perkins 1, 8,
Nick Stubbs 5, Tomasz Trojanowski 19, Suzanne Tucker 27, Ivonne Wierink 7, Serg
Zastavkin 14, Zurijeta 4.

Cover photograph: Shutterstock/Tomasz Trojanowski

Manufactured in China
CPSIA Compliance Information: Batch # WAS1102PK: For Further Information contact Rosen Publishing, New York, New York at 1-800-237-9932

# Contents

# Be Safe, Be Happy

To be healthy, you need to stay safe. You can help to look after yourself inside and outside your home. To do this, you need to know what is safe and what can be dangerous.

*Accidents can happen anywhere, but if you play safely, they are less likely to happen to you.*

4

Every year, several million children in the U.S. go to the hospital because of an accident at home.

*Many streets are busy, so stay with an adult.*

## Safe Places and People

By learning some simple tips you can avoid accidents and have more fun. It is also important to know who you can trust. You should be careful around some people, such as strangers.

## Emergencies

An **emergency** is when there is immediate danger. It could be when someone falls off a bike. This book will tell you what to do in an emergency.

# Safety at Home

Tidying up helps to stop accidents. You can easily trip over things left lying around and hurt yourself. Remember to keep the stairs clear, too.

- *Try to straighten up your toys and clothes when you have finished with them.*

**HEALTHY HINTS**

Be careful around glass windows and doors. If you fall against one, it could easily shatter and cut you.

## Shocking Stuff

Computers, televisions, and other machines work using **electricity**. Electricity is useful, but it can also be dangerous. It can give you an **electric shock**.

## Using Electricity Safely

*Never* put anything into an **electric** socket except a plug that fits it. Don't try to change a light bulb yourself. Ask an adult to do it for you. Putting a drink on top of anything that is electric is dangerous. If the liquid spills, it could give you an electric shock.

*Try to keep any drinks away from the television.*

# Safe from Poisons

Many products around the home are useful, but they can also be very dangerous. Some may contain **poisons** that could harm you if you put them in your mouth or they spill on your skin. Stay away from these products.

*It can be hard tell the difference between candy and poisonous **medicines**. Check with an adult before you touch anything.*

## HEALTHY HINTS

Only take a medicine when your parent or carer can help you. It is important that you take the right amount at the right time.

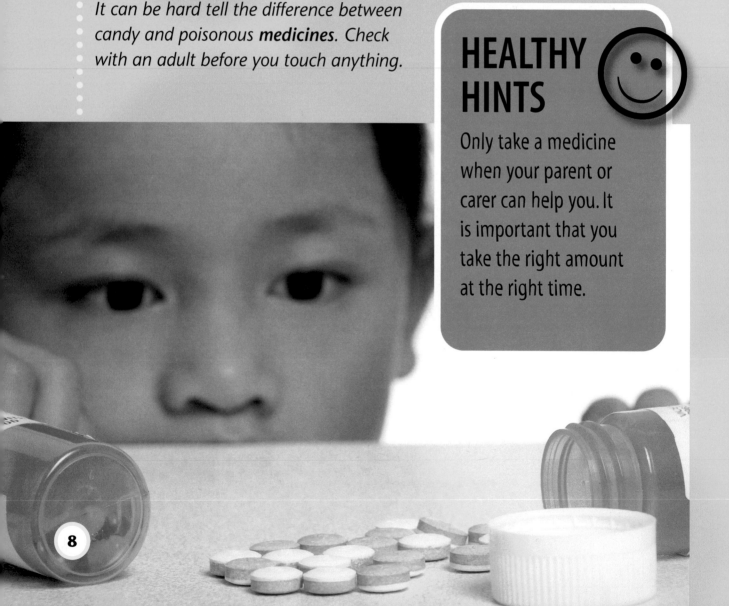

## Be Aware

Lots of products contain **chemicals** that you should not put in your mouth. Don't play with or eat perfumes, shampoos, and soaps. Paints and other decorating products are harmful, too. Tell an adult immediately if you or one of your friends has eaten something poisonous.

*If you see this symbol on a label, it tells you that the product is poisonous. Not all poisons have this symbol on them.*

# In the Kitchen

Learning how to prepare and cook food is fun when you know how to do it safely. There are some simple tips to follow to keep safe in the kitchen.

## Cooking

An adult should be with you when you cook. You can learn how to use the toaster or the blender, but remember that electrical things can be dangerous.

*Always ask an adult to show you how to use a knife safely.*

## Eating Sense

Don't eat while you're running around—you might choke. Sit down and eat your meal slowly. Make sure the food you eat is still fresh. Food that smells bad contains **germs** that may give you an upset stomach.

It's a Fact!

Storing food in the refrigerator keeps it fresh for longer.

*Spills on the kitchen floor make it slippery. Mop them up right away.*

# In the Yard and at the Park

It's a lot of fun to play outside. You can play in a playground or on a jungle gym in your backyard. Here are some tips to keep you safe while you have fun.

*Jungle gyms are made for safe climbing. It is safer to play on them than on trees and walls, which might break.*

## Swings and Slides

Hold on tight when you play on swings and other playground equipment. Be extra careful when it has been raining, because slides and seesaws will be slippery.

## Tools Are Not Toys

Gardening tools are for adults only. Many are sharp, because they are used for cutting and digging. Try to keep away from electrical tools, such as lawn mowers.

**HEALTHY HINTS**

Don't put plants or flowers in your mouth. They may be poisonous.

*Be careful on rope bridges and swings after it has been raining—they can be slippery.*

# Safe Places to Play

Always choose a safe place to play with your friends. The best places are yards, playgrounds, and parks, but try to make sure you go with an adult.

## Danger Spots

Some outdoor places, such as railroad tracks, are dangerous. Stay far away from them. Do not play on building sites or in empty buildings. You could easily fall onto something sharp or be hit by a falling brick or pole.

It's a Fact!

Every year, hundreds of U.S. children are injured trespassing on railroad tracks.

*Never play near railroad tracks. You could get an electric shock or be run over and killed by a high-speed train.*

14

## On the Farm

Farms are great places to visit, but you should only go there when you are with an adult. Farms have lots of dangerous machines and poisonous products. Big farm animals, such as cows, can also be dangerous.

*Visiting a farm for the day can be lots of fun. You might even get to feed some of the animals!*

# Fire!

Fires are dangerous. The smoke can make it difficult for you to breathe, and flames can spread through whole buildings very quickly.

## In the Kitchen

Many fires start in the kitchen. Frying food is dangerous because the hot fat and oil can catch fire.

Keep electric cords away from the stove and water. Heat from the stove could make the cord catch fire, and you could get an electric shock if it touches water.

*Never play with matches. You could start a fire.*

## Keep a Smoke Alarm

All homes should have smoke alarms. The alarm makes a loud noise when it detects smoke. Ask an adult to check that the smoke alarms in your home work.

*Firefighters spray water on a fire to put it out.*

# Road Safety

Roads are dangerous places. If you are hit by a car or other vehicle, you could be killed. If you follow some simple rules, you will stay safe.

## Crossing the Street

Always cross the street with an adult. Cross at a special crosswalk, or a safe place where you can see all the traffic. Stop at the **curb** and look left, right, and then left again. Walk straight across the street if it is clear. Keep looking and listening for traffic as you cross.

· · · · · · · · · · · · · · · · · · · ·

*It's safer to cross the street at a crosswalk.*

# On Your Bike

Always wear a cycle helmet and safety pads. Practice cycling in your backyard or at the park first. You can cycle on cycle paths and quiet roads when you feel ready, but only if an adult is with you.

## It's a Fact!

Wearing a seat belt in a car can stop you from being seriously injured in a crash.

*Wear a helmet and knee pads when you ride your bike to protect you.*

# Sun Safety

Some sunshine is good for you and keeps you healthy. Too much sunshine burns your skin and can damage it. This is sunburn and it can make your skin very sore.

*A sun hat shades your face and protects your head from the sunlight.*

## HEALTHY HINTS

Drink plenty of water in hot weather to replace the liquid you lose as you sweat. Add lots of ice to keep you cool!

# Sun Safety

- Put sunblock on if you are outside on a hot day. Sunblock shields your skin from the Sun's rays.
- Wear a hat and cover your arms with long sleeves. Loose clothes help to keep you cool.
- Bright sunlight can damage your eyes. Never look directly at the Sun and protect your eyes with sunglasses.
- The Sun's rays are strongest around 12 o'clock so stay inside at this time.

*Put sunblock on your skin every two hours and after you swim.*

# Water Safety

It's important to learn to swim so you can play safely with your friends in the water. An adult should always be with you when you are playing in the water.

*It's a lot of fun playing in a swimming pool if you follow a few safety rules.*

## HEALTHY HINTS

- Do not jump into the water near other people.
- Do not run around the swimming pool. You might slip.
- Stay in a depth of water that is comfortable for you.

## Don't Swim Here

It's not safe to swim in canals or in most rivers and ponds. They are often deep and may have **currents** that can sweep you away. In winter, the water at the surface may also freeze into ice.

*Never walk on a frozen river or pond. If the ice is thin, you could fall into the freezing water below and drown.*

# Stranger Danger

Most people are kind, but some people want to hurt children. Never talk to strangers when you are away from home, even if they seem friendly.

*Never wander off on your own when you are in a busy place.*

## HEALTHY HINTS

Learn your telephone number and carry two quarters with you. If you get lost while you are out, you will be able to call someone at home.

## What to Do

If a stranger talks to you, don't pay attention to them—walk away. Never go anywhere with someone who you don't know. Tell a parent, babysitter, or teacher if you are worried about a stranger.

## Busy Places

Stay close to the adult you are with in a crowded store or a busy street. If you do get lost, find an adult you can trust, such as a salesperson.

*It's fun to talk to your friends on the Internet, but never "talk" to a stranger. DO NOT give your name or address online.*

# First Aid and Emergencies

Accidents and emergencies sometimes happen. If you know what to do, you might save someone's life. **First aid** tells you how to help people who have had an accident.

When you call 911, the operator will ask you where you are and what has happened.

It's a Fact!

In an emergency, dial 911 and tell the operator what has happened.

## Small Accidents

You can treat some minor accidents at home. Slight burns should be held under cold water for 20 minutes. Small cuts can be cleaned and covered with a bandage.

## Serious Accidents

Serious accidents include:
- when someone has fallen and cannot move
- when someone is in pain or seems asleep
- when a cut is bleeding badly.

Tell an adult there has been accident right away.

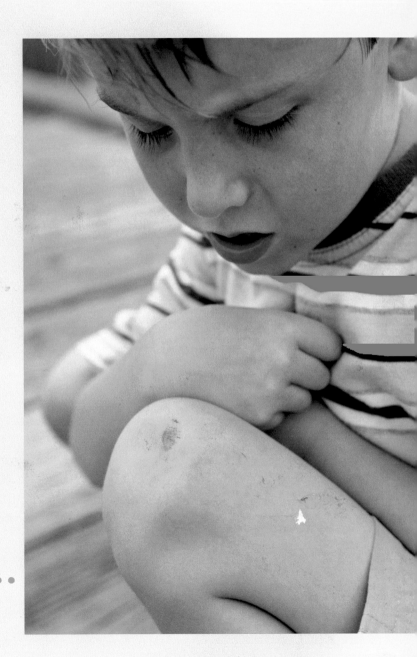

*Always clean a cut or graze before putting on a bandage.*

# Make a Safety Game

Make a board game about safety at home to play with your friends.

You will need:

- cardboard box
- a counter for each player
- 4 pieces of white paper
- 3 sheets of card
- colored pens
- scissors • glue
- pencil

1. To make the playing board, ask an adult to cut the side off of a cardboard box. Cover the cardboard with the sheets of white paper.

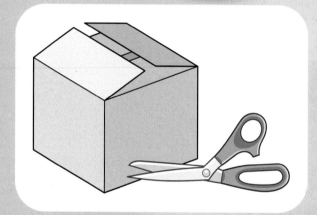

2. Draw the course the players will follow on the playing board. Divide it into 35–40 boxes and mark the ends "S" for Start and "F" for Finish.

3. Decorate the rest of the board to make it colorful and fun.

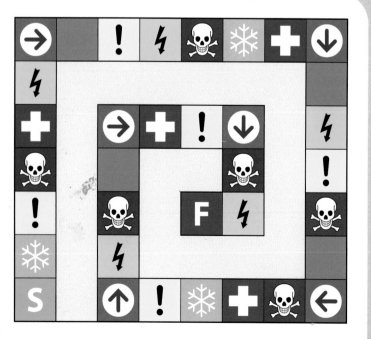

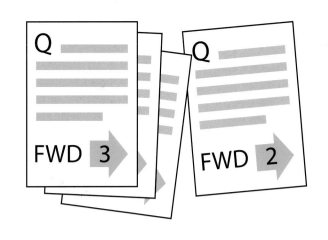

4. Divide each card into six equal boxes. Cut them out to make 18 question cards.

5. On each card, write a question about safety. Write the answer on the back. Write the number of spaces the player goes forward if they get the question right.

6. Place all the counters at the Start. Decide which player will go first. If the player gets the answer right, he or she moves forward. If not, the player stays where he or she is. The winner is the first person to reach the Finish.

Use this book to help you write the questions. For example: "A building is on fire. What should you do?" (Answer: "Leave the building, tell an adult, and call 911.")

# Keep Safe Topic Web

Use this topic web to discover themes and ideas in subjects that are related to keeping safe.

**GEOGRAPHY**
- Understanding which places in the local area are safe to play in and which places are dangerous.
- How to stay safe in water, in both swimming pools and natural water areas, such as the sea, rivers, and lakes.
- Draw a map of your local area and mark which areas are safe to play in and which areas might be dangerous.

**HEALTH EDUCATION**
- Stranger danger and how to keep safe.
- Understanding road safety.
- How to safely use the Internet.
- How to help others in an emergency or accident situation.
- The role of the police and fire department.
- Taking responsibility for personal safety and safety of others.

## KEEP SAFE

**ART AND DESIGN**
- How to design and make a safety game board, question cards, and counters from cardboard and paper.

**SCIENCE**
- How fires start and how to prevent them.
- Substances and medicines found in the home and how to stay safe around them.
- Understanding how the Sun can be harmful and how to stay safe in sunshine.
- How to prepare food safely.

# Glossary

**chemicals** substances in the body that affect how it behaves

**curb** the edge of the sidewalk beside a street

**currents** movements of water in the sea or a river or stream

**electric** made to work using electricity

**electric shock** a powerful shock from an electric current

**electricity** energy used to make machines work

**emergency** a dangerous event or situation

**first aid** help given to someone who is hurt

**germs** tiny living things that can cause diseases

**medicines** substances people take when they are sick

**poisons** substances that harm people

# Further Information and Web Sites

## Books

*Being Healthy, Feeling Great: Safety*
by Kate Purdie
(PowerKids Press, 2010)

*Keeping Safe*
by Slim Goodbody
(Gareth Stevens Publishing, 2007)

*Looking After Me: Safety*
by Liz Gogerly
(Crabtree Publishing, 2008)

*Watch Out!: At Home*
by Claire Llewellyn
(Barron's Educational, 2006)

## Web Sites

Due to the changing nature of Internet links, PowerKids Press has developed an online list of Web sites related to the subject of this book. This site is updated regularly. Please use this link to access this list:
www.powerkidslinks.com/hah/safe/

# Index